Parle Comme *Moi*
—*Talk Like Me*—

GW01390040

Dans le magasin de jouets

by
Stephen Power

Illustrated by
Richard Marshall

Bonjour

Hello

Before starting, say *Bonjour (child's name)* to the child. Prompt child to answer *Bonjour*…Do this by signaling with your hands and repeating if necessary, or just explain in English.

Preston, a brown teddy bear, had travelled all the way from England to a toyshop in Paris. He didn't know that he was in a different country. He was tired and wanted to rest. The shopkeeper put Preston on a shelf next to a yellow duck called Nancy.

'Bonjour !' said Nancy. Preston didn't understand this strange word. He didn't realise that Nancy was simply saying 'hello'. Nancy continued to speak. 'Je m'appelle Nancy.' More strange words, thought Preston. But Nancy was only telling Preston her name. Then she welcomed Preston to the shop.

'Bienvenue dans le magasin de jouets.'

Nancy asked Preston his name. 'Comment t'appelles-tu ?' Preston didn't understand.

'Comment t'appelles-tu ?' Nancy repeated. Preston still didn't understand and in any case he was feeling very sleepy.

Nancy was wondering why Preston wouldn't talk to her.

'Tu ne veux pas être mon ami ?' Nancy asked Preston. She wanted to know if Preston would be her friend. Preston still didn't reply. Nancy shook his shoulder.

'Oui ou non ?' Yes or no? she demanded. But Preston had fallen fast asleep.

Bonjour
Hello
Bon-zhoor

Je m'appelle…
My name is…
Juh ma-pel

Bienvenue dans le magasin de jouets
Welcome to the toyshop
Byah-ven-noo don luh ma-ga-za(n) duh joo-aay

Comment t'appelles-tu ?
What is your name?
Komon tapel tew

Tu ne veux pas être mon ami ?
Do you not want to be my friend?
Tew nuh vuh pah eh-truh mon amee

Oui ou non
Yes or no
Wee oo nohn

A lady came into the shop the following morning. 'Bonjour !' said the shopkeeper. Nancy straightened her hat. Nancy was desperate to leave the shop and was hoping a customer would buy her soon. Although Nancy thought Preston didn't want to be her friend, she still thought she had better warn him to smarten up. 'Arrange ton écharpe', said Nancy, pointing at Preston's scarf.

Preston didn't understand that Nancy was only telling him to tidy his scarf; he thought she was asking if she could have it. 'Arrange ton écharpe', Nancy repeated.

Preston didn't say anything – he didn't know what to say. He wanted to make friends but he was also very fond of his scarf. Nancy tried to tidy his scarf for him. Preston turned away sharply.

'Très bien', huffed Nancy. Nancy thought Preston couldn't be bothered to smarten himself up. 'Tu ne veux pas partir d'ici ?' Nancy asked. She wanted to know if Preston wanted to leave the toyshop. 'Oui ou non ?' she asked. Preston didn't understand Nancy but he was too shy to say so. He just shrugged his shoulders. The lady decided to take both Preston and Nancy. The shopkeeper put Preston and Nancy in a bag and said goodbye. 'Au revoir !'

'Oh revwar,' Preston said to himself. He had never heard anyone say 'goodbye' like this before.

Nancy was wondering how she was going to make friends with Preston if he wouldn't speak to her. Preston was wondering how he was going to make friends with anyone if he couldn't understand what was being said.

Bonjour
Hello
Bon-zhoor

Arrange ton écharpe
Tidy your scarf
*A-rohnge tohn
ay-sharp*

Très bien
Very well
Treh beeyah

**Tu ne veux pas
partir d'ici ?**
You don't want
to leave?
*Tew nuh vuh
pah parteer dissee*

Oui ou non
Yes or no
Wee oo nohn

Au revoir
Goodbye
Oh revwar

Merci

Thank you

The lady took Nancy and Preston to her house. The lady's daughter was waiting at the front door and shouted excitedly, but with more strange words that Preston didn't understand.

'Qu'est-ce que c'est, Maman ?' said the girl.

'It's a present for you,' said her mum. This time it was Nancy who didn't understand; she thought the girl's mum spoke in a very strange way. The girl thanked her mum. 'Merci, Maman. C'est un beau cadeau.'

At bedtime, the girl put Preston and Nancy on her pillow.

'Je m'appelle Sophie', said the girl. Preston guessed the girl was saying her name – Sophie. Preston realised that Sophie spoke like Nancy. Sophie's mum came into the bedroom.

'It's time to sleep now, Sophie.' More strange words, thought Nancy. Preston was sad. He felt left out because he didn't speak like Sophie and Nancy. Nancy was worried that she couldn't understand Sophie's mum.

Qu'est-ce que c'est, Maman ?
What's that, Mum?
Kess kuh say, Mah-mon

Merci, Maman
Thank you, Mum.
Mairsee Mah-mon

C'est un beau cadeau
It's a beautiful present
Say uh bo ka-doh

Je m'appelle Sophie
My name is Sophie
Juh ma-pel Sophie

Preston couldn't sleep because the window had been left open and he was cold. He went to close it. He stepped onto the window ledge to reach the window handle. But Nancy woke up.

'Qu'est-ce que tu fais ?' shouted Nancy. Preston didn't understand that Nancy just wanted to know what he was doing. He was so startled that he fell out of the window. Nancy went after him. She thought that Preston was hurt. She began to scream and shout because she was worried for him. But Preston thought Nancy was scared of something in the house. So he started to run. Nancy ran after him.

Preston raced through the dark streets. He didn't know Nancy was following behind. Preston stopped by an open window. Somewhere to rest, he thought. Preston had one foot through the window when he heard Nancy's voice.

'Qu'est-ce que tu fais ?' said Nancy. She could see that Preston didn't understand. So she simply asked him 'why?': 'Pourquoi ?' Preston thought Nancy wanted to go with him so he began to push her through the window. Nancy pleaded with Preston to stop. 'Arrête ! Arrête !' she wailed. 'C'est le magasin de jouets !' But Preston carried on pushing. Nancy landed on the floor with a bump and Preston came tumbling after. 'Mais, pourquoi ?' Nancy screamed. Preston didn't understand Nancy but he could sense she was angry. He now realised that Nancy hadn't wanted to go through the window after all. And Preston could see why. If only he had understood what Nancy had said when he was pushing her through the window: 'C'est le magasin de jouets !' – it was the toyshop! But it was too late to change things now; the shopkeeper had just locked the window.

Qu'est-ce que tu fais ?
What are you doing?
Kess kuh tew fay

Pourquoi
Why
Puh-kwah

Arrête
Stop
Ah-reht

C'est le magasin de jouets
It's the toyshop
Say luh ma-ga-za(n) duh joo-aay

Mais
But
May

Français

French

10

Nancy was angry and sad. Preston was annoyed too. 'I don't know why you're so upset,' said Preston. 'You didn't have to follow me.'

Nancy didn't understand Preston and she told him so. 'Je ne comprends pas', she shouted back. And she wanted to know why he was speaking so strangely.

'Pourquoi parles-tu bizarrement ?'

'I don't understand,' replied Preston. 'Why do you speak in a strange way?' Preston was very frustrated and so was Nancy; they just couldn't understand each other. A moose sitting on the shelf interrupted.

'Vous ne parlez pas la même langue', he said, looking at Nancy. The moose turned his head and looked at Preston and said exactly the same thing but in English. 'You don't speak the same language.' Preston and Nancy were amazed. Preston had understood the moose and so had Nancy.

The moose explained to Nancy that she spoke French. 'Tu parles Français.' And that Preston spoke English. 'Il parle Anglais.'

'You speak English,' he told Preston. 'And she speaks French, like everyone else in France. You are in Paris now, and Paris is in France.'

Je ne comprends pas
I don't understand
Juh nuh kom-prohn pah

Pourquoi parles-tu bizarrement ?
Why do you speak strangely?
Pu-kwah parl tew bizar-mohn(t)

Vous ne parlez pas la même langue
You don't speak the same language
Voo nuh parlay pah la mem long

Tu parles Français
You speak French
Tew parl fronsay

Il parle Anglais
He speaks English
Eel parl onglay

Preston hadn't realised he had actually travelled to another country. He didn't know about France and speaking French. It all seemed very complicated.

The moose tried to explain. 'Français – French. Anglais – English. Do you understand? Comprends-tu ?   Yes or no? Oui ou non ?'

'No,' said Preston.

'Non', said Nancy.

Preston and Nancy were still very confused.

'How do you know how to speak English *and* French?' asked Preston.

Nancy asked the very same question in French. 'Pourquoi parles-tu Anglais et Français ?'

The moose explained he was from Canada, a country where some people speak English and some speak French.

'My name is Ontario,' said the moose. 'Je m'appelle Ontario.'

'Je m'appelle Nancy', said Nancy.

Preston introduced himself too, only he tried doing it in French. 'Je m'appelle Preston.'

'Bravo !' said Ontario. 'Well done!'

Ontario helped Preston and Nancy talk to each other. Preston realised that Sophie was just like Ontario; she could speak English and French, she just preferred to talk in French. And Nancy now knew that Sophie's mum didn't speak in a special language so that Nancy wouldn't understand. She spoke in English, just like Preston.

Français
French
Fronsay

Anglais
English
Onglay

Comprends-tu ?
Do you understand?
Kom-prohn tew

Oui ou non
Yes or no
Wee oo nohn

Pourquoi parles-tu Anglais et Français ?
Why do you speak English and French?
Pu-kwah parl tew onglay aay fronsay

Je m'appelle...
My name is...
Juh ma-pel

Bravo
Well done
Bravoh

Au revoir

Goodbye

Preston promised to get Nancy out of the shop and back to Sophie.

'Mais comment ?' said Nancy. 'La fenêtre est fermée.'

'Nancy wants to know how you will get out when the window is closed,' said Ontario.

'There is another window,' said Preston defiantly.

'Qu'est-ce que tu dis ?' said Nancy. She wanted to know what Preston had said. Ontario explained as Preston pointed to an open window.

'Regarde ! Il y a une autre fenêtre', said Ontario. 'Elle est ouverte.'

'Mais elle est trop haute !' said Nancy.

'Nancy is right,' said Ontario. 'The window is too high. You can't get up there.'

However, Ontario had an idea and said he would help Preston and Nancy escape but only if he could go with them. Ontario's plan was to use a toy aeroplane to fly the three of them through the high window. Nancy and Preston agreed to Ontario's daring escape plan. 'Allons-y !' Nancy yelled as they squeezed onto the aeroplane.

'Oui, Nancy', said Ontario. 'Allons-y. Let's go.' The aeroplane started to move. 'Au revoir le magasin !' Ontario shouted, which he then repeated in English. 'Goodbye shop!' But the aeroplane wasn't strong enough to hold the three of them and it spun out of control, throwing Ontario, Nancy and Preston into a box below.

They were too tired to climb out and fell asleep.

Mais comment ?
But how?
May komon

La fenêtre est fermée
The window is closed
La fuh-netr aay fairmay

Qu'est-ce que tu dis ?
What did you say?
Kess kuh tew dee

Regarde ! Il y a une autre fenêtre. Elle est ouverte.
Look! There is another window. It is open.
Re-gar(d) ! Eel ya ewn oar-tre fuh-netr. El ay oo-vair

Mais elle est trop haute
It's too high
May el ay tro hoat

Allons-y
Let's go
Alohn-zee

Oui
Yes
Wee

Au revoir le magasin
Goodbye shop
Oh revwar luh ma-ga-za(n)

Preston, Nancy and Ontario woke up when they heard the noise of a van's engine. The box they had fallen into had a rocking horse inside. The rocking horse had been ordered by a customer that morning and was now being loaded onto the delivery van. Nancy feared she wouldn't see Sophie again. Ontario gave her a cuddle. 'Ne t'inquiète pas', said Ontario.

'What did you say, Ontario?' Preston asked.

'I was telling Nancy don't worry. Ne t'inquiète pas.'

'Don't worry,' said Preston. 'But we won't see Sophie again.' Ontario tried to cheer Preston up. 'This rocking horse will be going to another family,' he said. 'The delivery man will never know we're in here.'

'Qu'est-ce que tu dis ?' asked Nancy. Ontario was fed up of repeating himself. He suggested that Nancy learn English and Preston learn French.

'Will you teach me French?' asked Preston.

'Qu'est-ce que tu dis ?' Nancy interrupted.

'Preston wants me to teach him French,' said Ontario.

Nancy wondered if Ontario would teach her English.

'Pourrais-tu m'apprendre l'Anglais ?' she asked.

'Bien sûr. Of course,' said Ontario. 'Come on! Out of the box. Let's start now.' Ontario then started to clap his hands while repeating a little verse he had just made up:

> 'Let's go!
>
> Allons-y !
>
> Parle comme moi
>
> and talk like me!'

Read verse with rhythm.
Clap hands.
Repeat.
Try to get child to join in.

Ne t'inquiète pas
Don't worry
Nuh tank-ee-et pah

Qu'est-ce que tu dis ?
What did you say?
Kess kuh tew dee

Pourrais-tu m'apprendre l'Anglais ?
Could you teach me English?
Pooray tew ma-prohndre lohn-glay

Bien sûr
Of course
Beeyah sewr

Allons-y
Let's go
Alohn-zee

Parle comme moi
Talk like me
Parl kom mwa

1 un   2 deux   3 trois   4 quatre   5 cinq

6 six   7 sept   8 huit   9 neuf   10 dix

The first thing Ontario wanted to teach was parts of the body. 'Touch your arm,' said Ontario. Preston touched his arm. 'Touche ton bras', said Ontario. Nancy touched her arm.

Touche ton bras
Touch your arm
Toosh tohn bra

Point to body parts as you say them.

Pick out colours as you say them using objects in the room.

Ontario continued. He asked them to touch their hair, les cheveux *(lay shuh-vuh)*; head, la tête *(la teht)*; neck, le cou *(luh koo)*; nose, le nez *(luh ney)*; mouth, la bouche *(la boosh)*. Ontario then asked them to find colours amongst the toys. They had to touch something red, rouge *(rooj)*; and then something blue, bleu *(bluh)*; and white, blanc *(blon)*; and green, vert *(vair)*; and yellow, jaune *(joan)*.

Ontario then pulled a trampoline out of a box. He told Preston to jump ten times on the trampoline while Nancy counted:

0	1	2	3	4	5	6	7	8	9	10
Zéro	un	deux	trois	quatre	cinq	six	sept	huit	neuf	dix
Zay-roh	*uh*	*duh*	*trwa*	*kat-ruh*	*sank*	*sees*	*set*	*weet*	*nuhf*	*dees*

Suddenly, the doors of the van began to open. Nancy, Preston and Ontario were having such fun they hadn't realised the van had stopped. Nancy and Ontario scrambled back into the box with the rocking horse. Preston didn't have time to get down from the trampoline. He tried to jump towards the box but instead he hurtled towards some rubber balls. Luckily, he bounced off the balls and landed back in the box, right on top of Ontario and Nancy.

Regarde

Look

As the delivery man carried the box up the driveway to the house, Preston heard a child's voice. It was a little girl's voice and it sounded very familiar to Preston.

'Merci pour le cheval à bascule, Maman', mumbled the girl. The girl was thanking her mum for the rocking horse, but she didn't sound very excited. However, when the girl opened the box she shouted at the top of her voice.

'Regarde, Maman !'

The delivery man stared down at Preston, Nancy and Ontario. He couldn't understand how they had got into the box. But it was a nice surprise for Nancy and Preston. They looked up towards the girl and recognised her at once: it was Sophie.

Sophie picked up Nancy and Preston.

'Comment sont-ils arrivés dans cette boîte ?' said Sophie.

'Yes indeed,' said Sophie's mum, 'How did they get in that box?'

Sophie told her mum she didn't want the rocking horse now that she had Nancy and Preston back. 'Je ne veux plus du cheval à bascule.'

The delivery man was about to take the box away when Nancy realised that Ontario was still inside. She shook her head so that her hat fell off. She wanted it to fall in the box so that the others would see Ontario. But the hat fell to the floor.

Merci pour le cheval
à bascule, Maman
Thank you for the rocking horse, Mum
Mairsee por luh shuh-val ah bas- cuhl, Mah-mon

Regarde, Maman
Look, Mum
Re-gar(d), Mah-mon

Comment sont-ils arrivés dans cette boîte ?
How did they get in that box?
Komon son-teel areeve dohn set bwat

Je ne veux plus du cheval à bascule
I don't want the rocking horse anymore
Juh nuh vuh plew dew shuh-val ah bas-cuhl

'**V**ite !' Nancy whispered to Preston, 'Donne-moi ton écharpe.'

Preston knew this word: écharpe. It was French for scarf. Nancy still wants my scarf, thought Preston.

Preston remembered how to say *no* in French. 'Non !' he declared. He was very fond of his scarf.

'Oui', demanded Nancy.

'Non', said Preston.

'Oui', said Nancy.

Nancy managed to grab Preston's scarf. She tugged so hard that she fell from Sophie's arms. Luckily, Preston's scarf slipped off his neck and fell right into the box, just as Nancy had intended. The delivery man saw Ontario when he grabbed Preston's scarf. He asked if Sophie wanted the moose as well.

 'Oui, s'il te plaît', said Sophie.

At bedtime, Sophie put Nancy in one corner of her bed, Preston in the other and Ontario in the middle and then wished them goodnight.

'Bonne nuit !' said Sophie.

'What did she say?' Preston whispered to Ontario.

'Goodnight,' said Ontario.

'Sorry,' said Preston. 'It's late. I didn't think. Goodnight...'

'No,' Ontario interrupted. 'Sophie said *goodnight* in French: bonne nuit.'

'Qu'est-ce que tu dis ?' said Nancy.

Ontario sighed. He was fed up of repeating everything.

Nancy was looking forward to learning more English. Preston was looking forward to learning more French. Ontario could only think about how busy he was going to be.

	Vite
	Quick
	Veet
Non	Oui
No	Yes
Nohn	*Wee*

Donne-moi ton écharpe
Give me your scarf
Dohn mwa tohn ay-sharp

Oui, s'il te plaît
Yes please
Wee, seel-tuh-play

Bonne nuit
Goodnight
Bon nwee

Qu'est-ce que tu dis ?
What did you say?
Kess kuh tew dee

23

Learn with Ontario

Let's see what you have learned. Answer oui ou non.

Tu t'appelles Ontario ? Prompt... Je m'appelle..

Tu parles Anglais ?

Tu as deux bras ?

Tu as une tête ?

Tu as trois nez ?

Nancy est jaune ?

L'écharpe de Preston est rouge ?

(Point to a window) La fenêtre est fermée ?

BRAVO ! Tu parles comme moi.

Au revoir

Goodbye!

Prompt child to say Au revoir.

24